The Rookie Truck Driver

Based On A True Story

Percy Smith

Contents

1.
2.
3.
4.
5.
6.

Thank you for purchasing my book. My purpose for writing this book is to tell the story of my first year driving a tractor trailer over the road. I want to help you, as the reader, decide whether or not driving commercial vehicles is for you. Before getting my CDL I was lost and had no direction, no clue about what steps to take to get my license. Like you may be feeling now, I wish I had someone that could help me out with the process.

I made it through the training, but there are many people that never go through with getting their license because they don't know how to. I'm here to help. I hope you enjoy my journey and find the checklist I have provided at the end to be useful. I do not mention the actual companies that have employed me for legal reasons, but please don't hesitate to contact me via email or Instagram with any questions, I'll be glad to answer them all!

E mail: rookiextrucker@gmail.com
Follow me on Instagram: @totaxperkp

Chapter 1
Thoughts About Becoming A Trucker

I

woke up one Thursday morning, logged into the bank app on my phone and checked my latest direct deposit. A frown appeared on my face. I was seriously feeling fed up of the salary I was making biweekly at my job. $700 every two weeks wasn't enough, especially living in Miami. I needed to make a change, quickly. I got some good advice from a friend who worked with me; " *why don't you just get your CDL?* " .

At the time, I was addicted to marijuana and did not want to let the habit go. Her advice kept replaying in my head for weeks, until one day I just said " *fuck I'm going to do it.* " I made the decision to better my life.

But there was a problem, I didn't know where to start. I started watching videos on YouTube about getting a CDL license.

Truckers were explaining I needed to pass three written tests before obtaining my permit and that I should do so before signing up to attend a CDL school. So that's exactly what I did. An associate told me about an app called *DMV Genie* that I could use to study for all the tests.

I spent a few days studying one test at a time, before heading to the DMV when I felt confident that I would pass. I passed all three tests on the first try; air brakes, combination, and general knowledge. The DMV clerk told me I needed to pass a DOT physical to obtain my permit. Next I googled *"DOT physician near me"* and found a physician near my home to take my DOT physical, that cost $60.

The DOT physician checked my pulse, blood pressure, vision in both eyes, and hearing. I also had to pass a urinalysis test. All together it took about 30 minutes to complete and afterward the physician provided me with A DOT card. I immediately went back to the DMV to show I had received the card, The DMV clerk handed me a permit and stated that I could not get behind a commercial vehicle wheel to drive until 15 days after receiving the permit.

Now that I had my permit and DOT physical In hand, I was ready to find a CDL school near my home, sign up, and attend.

There were two schools near my home, I checked both of them out to see which one had the best learning environment. The first one I checked was not well organized and it felt very uncomfortable, my instincts were telling me this school was not the one and to go elsewhere, that's exactly what I did.

I left and drove to the next one, this school was more organized and I felt more comfortable being there. I lived a couple blocks away so the location was very convenient for me to attend. I met with an advisor to go over the scheduled hours, how much it will cost me, and when I could start.

I decided to attend school full time 7am thru 5pm, Monday - Saturday so that I could complete the 160 hours in 4-5 weeks. These hours are required to be considered for employment at any trucking company.

The cost varies each season so I can't give an exact amount how much it will cost for you, you would have to walk in and speak with one of the advisors yourself. Some good advice I can give however, is if you have the money saved then pay it in full instead of taking out a loan. You'll save money, the price will be cheaper overall, and you won't be in debt.

Two weeks after I signed on the dotted line I began school. I had to sacrifice the 9-5 job I had in good faith that things would work out and use the remaining paid time off I accumulated to better myself.There was no failing in my eyes, I had to learn a new skill and learn it fast. The fact that I'd already received my permit and a DOT physical saved me a lot of frustration. During the first week of school there was a lot of information to take in. They tell you to go to the DMV, take the 3 written tests, and get a physical in order to receive a permit and all within 7-10 days. You cannot get inside of the tractors to learn how to drive until you get the permit and DOT physical.

The first two weeks of school was in a classroom, the instructor was a woman who's been driving trucks for many years. I learned about pre-trip/post-trip procedures, paper logs, understanding a commercial vehicle map, truck stops/ how to fuel, the DOT regulations, the DO's & DON'Ts while on the road, uphill & downhill grades, military time, and much more.

It's a lot of helpful information that's taught so have your eyes and ears ready to learn.

The pre-trip material had to be the most stressful subject. You basically have to learn everything about the truck and trailer. The best way to learn is YouTube searching "Class A pre trip" is a good place to start. There you will find plenty of videos to choose from, just find the one that suits you and watch it everyday, apply what they teach you during school and you'll be fine.

On the 4th of July I got a phone call from a recruiter, she asked me if I was interested in driving for their company. I pulled out a sheet of paper the CDL school gave me with questions I should ask any recruiter who calls me about employment. I liked the responses she was giving me and I took into consideration that it would be my first trucking job. What made The company stand out from any other company that called was the fact that they would pay for me to get to and from Miami on a plane when driving out of state, since there's no operating center in Florida. She sent over an application to my email and informed me to fill it out and in 2-3 days she would get back to me to see if I'm qualified to work, but I knew I would be as I had no criminal background and a good driving record. The only thing I was skeptical about was the drug test. She told me that they perform two types of drug screening; hair follicles and urine. As I mentioned, I was previously a daily marijuana smoker, but stopped before I started the CDL school to make sure I would be clean to get my DOT physical card. I read up about the hair follicle test and it stated that it may take 90 days or more to get out of my hair roots. But I didn't let that stop me, I prayed that no signs of marijuana would come up when it was time for me to take the screening. I briefly spoke with other companies but for some reason I felt I should stick with the first company that called. I was all in!

I took a week off to go visit my son, as he stays with his mom in another state. It was a well needed mini vacation and I had so much fun with him. I gained even more motivation from spending time with my son and soon I was ready to get back home and back to school to finally learn how to drive a tractor trailer. Man, it was one hell of a learning curve.

The range is the yard of land that the school uses to teach students about the pre trip/post trip, coupling and uncoupling, and backing maneuvers. The instructor broke the class up into groups so that everyone would get a chance at learn hands on.

We started off learning about Pre trips. You have to memorize different parts of the tractor and trailer. The test is graded based on the number of parts you name correctly. You don't know what part of the truck or trailer you are going to be tested on until the day of your test. They break it down into three parts:

A - the front of the truck & engine compartment.
B - the side of tractor and middle.
C - the entire trailer.

Next was Coupling and uncoupling. Me and four other guys took turns coupling and uncoupling. The concept is very easy but missing one step can ruin you and your driving record. It'll be considered a preventable accident on your DVR report. For instance, if you're uncoupling and you forget to drop the landing gear, the trailer will drop to the ground.

After that came straight line back, jack-knife parking, and alley docking. The key point here is to *ALWAYS USE BOTH MIRRORS AND BACK UP AS SLOWLY AS POSSIBLE.*

Straight line backing - this is when you pull forward with the tractor trailer and back up in a straight line. While backing up, if you want the tail of the trailer to go left you have to steer right, and for it to go right, you have to steer left.

Jack-knife parking - when you pull forward with the tractor trailer and, as you start backing up, you change lanes either from left to right or from right to left.

Alley docking - when you have to back up and park the trailer. This, by far, was the hardest maneuver of them all.

It was so difficult for me to understand all the maneuvers at first because I was so used to driving a car, but eventually I got the concept and it is now a piece of cake for me.

Driving on the road with the instructor and learning how to shift gears was another thing that blew my mind. Never in my life had I driven a manual transmission car, so I knew nothing about shifting gears. I remember my first time shifting gears I didn't understand the concept of double clutching. You have to push the clutch down into neutral and then again to shift into the next gear. The more I missed the gear, the more it sounded like the transmission was about to fall out the bottom of the truck!

The instructors were hardly "Mr. nice guy" and at times it seemed like they were trying to ruin my confidence, but they do that to make you learn faster, and it actually works. Its funny now when I look back at it, but while learning could you imagine a guy in your ear telling you that " *you're a total fuck up* " and asking " *maybe driving a tractor trailer isn't for you?* " I went home to practice shifting and double clutching with a plunger every night until I finally got it, it was an overwhelming feeling once I finally learned how to shift.

In cab brake test - I actually didn't learn the in cab brake test until the day before my pre trip testing. I was so busy learning about everything else that it slipped my mind that this was a part of the pre trip test. I practiced on a tractor that wasn't being used, I stayed inside the truck one day on the range for about two hours practicing the steps. After class was over I went home and wrote down every step of the test on a white erasable board that's on my bedroom wall. I kept repeating the steps out loud to myself, until I eventually knew them by heart.

As you can see, there are a lot of things to learn in a matter of 4-5 weeks but **<u>YOU CAN DO IT</u>** . Put your mind to the challenge and execute. Time is something you can never get back, so don't waste it, you can do whatever you put your mind to so believe in yourself!

Pre-trip testing day - I woke up that morning energized and ready for the test. I spent the first part of my day looking at videos on YouTube of the Pre-trip, reading my white board, and recapping the steps of the in cab brake test. I eventually felt overwhelmed and needed a way to calm down. My phone rang and it was a friend of mine, she asked me if I was ready for the test, I said yes but that I was a little overwhelmed and needed to calm down. She made her way to my house and we had sex to calm my nerves.I must say, it was well needed. I went to school afterwards and passed the test on my first try. During the hour break they gave us I called to thank her, she laughed and asked why I was thanking her. I told her because of the sex we had, I believe it played a big part in me passing the test, and I still believe that..

A couple days later it was time to take the backing maneuvers test and the road test. By this time I was comfortable with all the maneuvers and with driving on the city roads. My shifting skills improved, and I passed my test with flying colors. I called everybody important to me and told them I'd passed all my tests. I was proud of my accomplishment. I received the papers I needed to take to the DMV to get my CDL class A driver's license. It was an amazing feeling to walk into the DMV the next morning to get my license. The process was well worth all the hard work, this is something nobody can take from me, but myself by making bad decisions. I'm thankful that I was able to put myself into a position to make more money and provide for me and my son.

Chapter 2
New Employment

fter completing school I had to get a paper from the office to take to the DMV which stated that I had completed 160 hours of training at an accredited CDL school. The DMV printed out my license, then I had to go back to the office to get my diploma -proof that I am now eligible to drive a commercial class A vehicle.

Next I called the recruiter to let her know I've completed school and that I have my license in hand, she told me congratulations and asked if I was ready to go through three weeks of training. Of course, I said yes. So we then discussed what date I would be able to fly into Green Bay, Wisconsin to start training. She let me know that the hotel would provide breakfast and the company operating center would provide lunch, thoughI would have to provide my own dinner. I still had to put my two weeks notice in at my current job, so I ended up starting two weeks from the date I got my license.

Note that before attending any company training make sure you have money saved up to eat for the duration. You will need to provide for yourself!

In between the two weeks I received an email from the recruiter with information; my plane ticket, hotel info, and instructions on how I was going to get from the Wisconsin airport to the operating center.

Week 1 - I made it to Green Bay, Wisconsin on a Friday. I had to call a cab service to pick me up and take me to the hotel, though this was paid for fully by the company. I ended up being roommates with a Hispanic guy named Julio. We attended the same school, but he finished before me because I had taken a week off to visit my son.

Training started the following Monday, I didn't know what to expect. I was still in shock that I had changed careers in the matter of a month.

First thing of course was some paperwork to sign, drug screening to complete, and the setting up of direct deposit.

The instructor informed us what would happen in the following weeks of training and that, in order to drive for the company, we would have to learn the company way of driving a 53 foot commercial vehicle. They taught a different strategy than the school on how to alley dock, what not to do while driving, and learning how to use A Qualcomm. Luckily, they gave out papers with steps on how to do a Pre-trip/ post trip inspection, in-cab air brake test, and coupling/uncoupling.

I had to pass a road test and complete the backing maneuver correctly to move on to week 2 - which was actually going out on the road with a trainer for an entire week delivering loads.

I ended up failing my road test the first time, though surprisingly they gave me another try to pass and I wasn't going to fail this time. I put my mind to the test, corrected every mistake I'd made on my first try, and I passed. It was a relief to know that I was moving on to the next stage of training.

Week 2- It was a Sunday and I was patiently waiting in my hotel room on a phone call from the trainer that I was to go on the road with, for a whole week. He called late Sunday and told me to meet him in the break room at the operating center the following day at 08:00am. His name was Dave and he was an older guy in his mid 40's. He'd been driving for a couple of years before switching over to become a trainer. He seemed like a cool person and we instantly got along, so from the jump I had a feeling this second week of training wasn't going to be so bad.

He had a brand new 2019 automatic freight-liner truck, the inside of which he kept well organized. There was a refrigerator and he even had a spare sleeping bag for me to use since I forgot to purchase my own.

His job was to watch my every move while driving and make sure I learned about logging my hours on the Qualcomm. Qualcomm is a grey tablet-like device that has a GPS installed within it.It keeps track of all work assignments and hours of service, as well as functioning as a messaging system to communicate with the driver business leaders, thereby reducing the need for drivers to call in for help.

Dave showed me step-by-step everything I needed to know about becoming a professional truck driver. I drove everyday. Dave stated that if I was tired from driving he would take over, but I didn't let that happen. I wanted to get all the experience I could, since I was only going to be out with him for 5 days.

I was catching on quickly and he was very impressed, particularly with my lack of fear to put the truck on cruise control.He told me that previous trainees were scared to go 63 miles per hour on cruise control. The only problem I had was alley docking. I wasn't comfortable with it yet, so he took over a couple of times to teach me different ways to back into docks, and I thanked him for that.

We also talked about what type of account I would be working. He was an OTR driver before becoming a trainer. I told him I'll be working a "jet set" account - which means that I wouldn't have a truck to myself like he does,because I live in Miami, Florida and there's no operating center in Florida. This meant that I wouldn't be able to have a refrigerator in my truck, so I would have to spend more money on food daily.

The week went by fast. On the last day of driving with Dave he pulled out the list of things I was being graded on throughout the week. I was scored on a scale of 1-5, and in nearly every section he gave me a 5.I did a great job and passed to continue on to week 3. He told me I was one of the best trainees he'd ever trained and that he had a feeling I was going to become a trainer myself one day. Dave liked that I was a good listener, caught on quickly, and corrected the simple mistakes I made whilst driving day by day. When we finally got back to the operating center I gathered my things and we shook hands. He wished me luck and told me I was going to do great, I told him I appreciated the great training but that I wasn't going to lie...and was glad it was over!Being watched continuously like that for five days felt so weird, i wanted to listen to some rap music while driving but I knew it would give old Dave a headache. I called a cab and headed back to the hotel to enjoy my 2 day weekend, because the third week of training started the following Monday.

The next morning I went outside the hotel to get some fresh air and ran into a couple of guys who were in training with me. We started to talk about how our weeks out on the road with our trainers had gone. A couple of them were complaining about their trainer, saying they didn't get along very well. According to one, their trainer had them driving for too long and another said that they were too hard on them for no reason. I, on the other hand, had one of the best experiences and have no complaints at all. My theory is that we as humans create our own problems. Think positive and do what's required to succeed, the more a person complains the more problems are created. Smiling and creating happiness is the only way to succeed.

Week 3- This was it, the last week of training, which consisted of learning how to use the Qualcomm, more hours of service, bill of ladings, and map reading. The instructor was tough on us all; stating that he will not tolerate any nonsense, no falling asleep in class, and no cell phones - either turn them off or put them on silent. He did not want to be distracted.

I suck at reading maps so I knew it would be difficult for me, but luckily map reading was not a requirement to pass week three. What was a requirement was learning how to operate the Qualcomm and the importance of the bill of lading. It was like learning how to use a computer for the first time, back in the early 2000's. I learned so little about the Qualcomm while with my trainer, because he was mostly operating it and it was a rushed environment so I never really got to grips with the information fully.

Everyday he gave us map reading homework. A couple of guys teamed up in the lobby of the hotel to find the answers to the questions the instructor gave out for homework. Some guys caught on, whilst easily some didn't...I was one of them. Nothing about map reading interested me, so I didn't care about it. Everytime I opened the map atlas book I would get sleepy, thank god it was only homework.

The last day of training was on a Friday, I packed my luggage and the rest of my belongings from my hotel room and took it with me to the operating center. All that was left was the Qualcomm test to determine if I would become a company driver, or if I would be going back to Miami and I damn sure was not going back to Miami. I passed the test and received my certificate of completion for the three weeks of training. It was a wonderful feeling, I felt accomplished.

I met with my driver business leader, who went over everything ahead, starting the following Monday. The truck they assigned to me was stationed in Carlisle, PA. I had to fly out from Green Bay, Wisconsin to Pennsylvania and, once I got there I wouldn't be able to start driving until I take a 10 hour DOT break.

I didn't know what to expect but I was ready for all the rookie challenges that were about to come my way.

I

t was a long day with me having to catch two flights which didn't get me into Pennsylvania until around 11:30 that night. I had to wait for my luggage and for the cab driver to get to the airport to pick me up. It took the guy about 30 mins to reach me, so by that time it was

12:30am and man, was I tired. I'd finally made it to the Carlisle operating center around 1am in the morning.

Once I made it there I honestly didn't know what to do or expect next. Dragging my luggage behind me, I went inside to the front desk and asked lady say there

"Good evening, I'm here to pick up my truck that I was assigned; tractor #48592"

She searched for the keys, but could not find them. She looked up the location of the truck and saw that it wasn't in Pennsylvania yet... it was parked in Virginia and still assigned to another driver. She informed me that he wasn't going to make it to Carlisle, PA until tomorrow evening.

What a bummer! I thought to myself, it was 1am in the morning and I was so tired from taking flights all day, all I wanted to do was get some sleep. I had to get a hotel room, though it was paid for by the company. I waited for the same cab driver who dropped me off to come back to pick me up, and he took another 30 minutes. The hotel was about 15 mins away andI was literally falling asleep while the guy was driving, so whatever he was talking to me about I wasn't listening.

I checked in and, thankfully, I had a room all to myself with no roommate, just me and two beds. My plan was to call my DBL in the morning to get an update about when to return to the operating center. I took a hot shower and fell asleep in minutes. The next morning, my DBL called me with an update about the truck I was assigned. She told me it would be at the Carlisle operating center that Saturday, late in the evening, so I was told to just stay at the hotel until Monday morning. That was okay with me since I had a hotel room all to myself, I actually was able to watch my little brother's first college game of the season on TV. The hotel provided breakfast, and nearby there was a Chili's and a Cracker Barrel so I enjoyed nice dinner meals. I quickly got bored so I took some time to read the guides I received while in training. Next I went to the hotel gym to get a work out in and afterwards I caught an Uber to Walmart to get a couple of things I needed for the road. Sunday morning I called my DBL again to ask how I would get to the Operating center Monday morning, she informed me that the hotel had a shuttle that would drop me off.

Sunday night I couldn't really sleep, it felt like the night before the first day of school but this was the first day of driving a tractor trailer solo, with no trainer! I actually started driving on my birthday, no celebration, just a focused hard working day ahead of me.

I woke up around 5am to be ready to catch the hotel shuttle back to the Operating center at 6am. I received the keys from the front desk clerk and headed to the truck.

Once I logged into the Qualcomm there was already a pre-assignment waiting for me, I was actually late as my appointment time was at 08:00am and about 25 miles away.

It was already about 07:15am so I went on duty/ pre trip which would take me approximately 30 mins to complete. The truck was in good condition, but had very low fuel so I decided to fuel up at the operating center. I drove to the fuel lanes to find out my fuel card did not work at the pump. I'm thankful I didn't leave the Operating center, I would've been stuck like glue if I'd left without a new fuel card. I received another card from the front desk, called the 1800 number to activate it, fueled the truck, and I was on my way.

I informed my DBL that I was running late, which is the last thing a driver wants to tell their DBL. Being late sucks, depending on how busy the customer is that day they might reschedule the load, or make a driver wait longer than expected, which would eat up the 14 hour clock.

I had to bobtail to a Marshall's distribution center to pick up an empty trailer, then take it to a Lowe's distribution center to drop it off and pick up a loaded trailer. Most companies want an empty trailer in exchange for a loaded trailer like this.

This load wasn't going far, it was a short run of only 60 miles. I made it to my destination in an hour, checked in with security at the guard shack, dropped the load in the location they told me to, picked up an empty one, completed all my paperwork and already another pre assignment was awaiting me.

My next load was a live load, which means that the company dock workers are going to load up the empty trailer once a driver arrives. When I got there, the line of trucks was almost around the corner and at that point I knew I was going to be waiting for a while. Surprisingly, the loaders didn't take long and they had me on my way in two hours. This load was a 150 mile run, that's a 3 hour drive with a tractor being governed at 63 miles per hour.

Managing the 14 and 11 hour clocks is very important, you don't want to run all the hours out to 0. Leaving 3-4 hours left on the clock after each day will help with the 70 hour clock when you're running low. The 3-4 hours you leave each day will roll over, meaning you'll gain back hours without having to do a reset (Going off duty for 34 hours).

It rained all day in Pennsylvania that day, and the streets were very slippery so I kept a good following distance between me and every car ahead of me. The three hour drive would leave me with 5 hours left on my 11 hour driving clock and 6 hours on my 14 hour on-duty clock. All I had to do was drop the trailer, then find a safe place to park for the night for a 10 hour break.

I finally reached the exit, but the GPS froze on me and I ended up missing my turn. Wow, was that a scary moment for me...I had to find a place to turn around. I was so upset at the Qualcomm for freezing on me, as I kept driving for over 20 minutes and still couldn't find a safe place to turn around. I started to get frustrated and made a bad decision to turn on a street that was too small.The right side of the trailer hit a guardrail, and would've fallen into a pond if I had kept going forward. It felt like my entire soul left my body, I thought I was going to be terminated indefinitely for sure.

I put my hazard lights on, turned the truck off,called the emergency maintenance hotline and told the operator what happened.

The guardrail was bent, but there was no damage to the trailer and luckily a guy pulled over to help stop traffic so that I could back up. It turned out to be barely half a mile ahead that I could have turned into safely to turn around! I ended up getting a ticket that cost me $350 and 3 points on my license.

By the time the cop left the site I only had 1 hour left on my 14 hour clock and I needed to find somewhere to park. There were no truck stops nearby, and I ended up parking at a motel. I was upset with myself, tired, hungry, and needed a shower so I booked a room, walked to the gas station to get a hot dog, took a shower, and fell asleep.

I didn't know what to expect the next morning when I got a phone call from my DBL about my accident and not making it on time for my appointment.

She asked me what happened and I explained it to her. She understood and gave me great advice to never turn down narrow streets, just keep going forward, no matter how long it takes to find a safe place to turn around.

As the weeks went on I got better at backing, maneuvering the trailer, managing my hours, and learning about the trucking industry in general.

Chapter 4
Quarter 1 - The Winter Season

T

ime was flying, by December I'd been driving for four months and have learned so much already.. From managing my 70 hour clock, to finding different ways to alley dock, driving in snow and, most importantly how to control a tractor trailer. The in's and out's of being a company driver are basic and it is generally a great experience but, of course, there are good and bad days that nobody can control. All drivers hate bad days because if you are not driving you aren't getting paid, and that sucks.

I went home to Miami for a couple of days during the Christmas and New Year holidays to spend time with my family. I knew when I returned to work in January that quarter 1, which is winter, would be in full effect.

I landed in Atlanta, GA, to pick up my tractor that I would be driving for the next couple of months. I had a new mindset for the new year and that was to save more money. Cut back on buying stuff I want and only buy things I need. Back when I was in training an older guy gave me some advice; *"save $100 every week you get paid and by the end of the year you would have saved $5200"* . He told me he'd been driving tractors for over 20 years, now he was getting into the owner operator program the company was offering. I took his advice and ran with it but I wanted to save 3 times more than $5200. After paying my bills and paying for food, I planned on transferring the rest from my checking into my savings account, and It's working perfectly for me. Self discipline is very important!

An active load I was assigned to drive to Ohio, where the temperature was in the negatives, was coming in from Miami. I'd never experienced such cold weather, the windshield wipers would start to freeze up, then ice builds up on the blades which makes the wipers useless. If the snow continues to fall, there is no way to have a clear view of the streets, so my best bet was to park at the closest truck stop and contact my DBL stating that I don't feel safe driving in those conditions. That's considered a bad day because, of course, I won't be getting paid, but my safety is more important.

I had a couple incidents where I almost bust my ass trying to walk on black ice, That was a sign that I should start wearing those ice cleats the company provided. The cleats were stretchable and went right over my steel toe boots. I put them on plenty of times while at truck stops and delivering loads.The black ice is very dangerous and can cost the company slip and fall injuries. I woke up the next morning to start my day, it was -10 degrees, my brakes on my tandem tires were frozen so the trailer would not move when I tried to start driving. I didn't know what to do so I called the emergency maintenance hotline to get a resolution. The operator told me to hit the brakes with a hammer to knock the ice off and it worked.

It was freezing but there was no snowfall. so it was safe to drive. The snow removers did a great job clearing out the roads but I didn't want to drive fast , since it was still dangerous and black ice can appear at anytime. I made it to my drop location, but they wouldn't accept the load because I had missed the appointment due to the snowstorm the previous day. They told me I would have to reschedule, which sucked because it was Sunday and I knew nobody in customer service was working and I wasn't going to get an update any time soon. So I found the nearest truck stop to park for the night and, as I expected, I didn't get an update until the next morning about the loads appointment. It eventually turned into a relay drop (when a driver drops the load at a company owned or rented drop lot for another driver to finish the load).

I thought driving in snow would be a hard task in a tractor but it really isn't, keeping my eyes on the road and paying attention to what's ahead will prevent any driver from causing an accident. When an accident occurs, you will have to take a urine drug test for the Department of Transportation, So stay drug free - you don't want to lose a great opportunity over drugs and alcohol!

The winter is no joke, you have to be prepared when it comes to staying warm. The bunk heater is small and is no good in temperatures under 40 degrees. I slept with two covers, socks, and sometimes even a jacket. I was very uncomfortable, but I got through it.

Stay strong rookie trucker and drive safely through the snow!

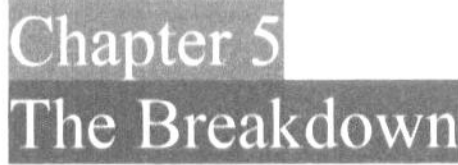

Chapter 5
The Breakdown

The chances of me having a perfect week were slim, meaning getting over 2500 miles without a truck breakdown. From my experience, every week there will be at least a day or two that will not go well. Here's a couple of my scenarios.

In March, with spring slowly approaching, the temperatures were still in the mid 40's. On a Tuesday I spent the night at the Pennsylvania operating center. I received a pre assignment that night to pick up a relay and drive it to a location to get live unloaded the next morning.

The location was around the corner from the operating center so I didn't have to drive far. I made it there on time, walked inside to give the shipper the bill of lading paperwork, then he told me to write my number on a sheet of paper and that they'd call me when a door is available for me to back in to get unloaded.

I waited for about 20 mins then eventually got a call telling me what door to back into, and when I got the green light the unload would be complete then I could come inside to get my paperwork.

It took them about an hour to unload me, the green light came on and I walked inside. The clerk stated " there are 4 pallets that we are refusing" I looked at him with a stale face and said "what do you mean, why are you refusing 4 pallets?".

"You have to contact your company about that" is what he told me. At that moment I knew my day was not going to be good.

I was curious to see what he was talking about, I jumped into my truck and pulled forward, I got out of the truck and walked to the back of the trailer. The four pallets they refused were cat food which were poorly shrink wrapped, causing them to tilt over and damage other products as well.

I contacted my DBL about the situation. I ended up having to submit a spill claim, take pictures of the pallets, and speak with driver services inside the operating center on where to drop the trailer in the yard. All together that situation had taken four hours from my 14 hour clock, and I had driven about 4 miles that day!

My next pre assignment was 30 miles away, it was a drop and hook so no big deal, but there was 1 problem; The load was to be delivered in New Jersey. In the north east, finding overnight parking and truck stops are very limited especially late in the day and I did not want to be in a situation where I had nowhere to park overnight. So I picked up the load and headed back to the operating center to sleep for the night.

Wednesday morning I got up early to start heading to New Jersey. As I was driving an update on my route came thru the MCP200 navigation, but I ignored it and kept on driving which was a big mistake. Once I got to the shipper they denied my load and told me I would have to reschedule because I was late. The load was supposed to be there at 02:00am, if I would have pulled over safely and checked the update on my route I would've seen the update to drop the load at a Pennsylvania drop lot, because it had been switched to a relay, since I was late. I even received a message on my tablet stating the update, but I ignored it. So I had to backtrack about 30 miles to Pennsylvania to drop the load, a lot of time wasted on my behalf.

So, in two days I'd had only driven about 200 miles. I'd usually have already driven at least 600 miles in two days, needless to say... my week started off terribly.

But, just as I thought it couldn't get any worse IT DID.

As I left a shipper in the New Jersey area from getting live loaded,I stopped and parked at a service area on the I-95 turnpike to grab something to eat. When I got back inside the tractor to start it up there was a problem; I couldn't go past 5 miles per hour on the odometer. I knew something wasn't right, so I parked my truck and called emergency maintenance to see if I could get a solution without having to get towed to a freight liner for repairs.

The representative told me that my truck was going thru a "5 MPH limit lock" which meant I would have to get it towed to the nearest freight liner for repairs. That was the last thing I wanted to hear, it was a Friday and my DBL doesn't work on the weekends, which means I'm left dealing with the weekend DBL's.

It was freezing in New Jersey that night, it had taken the tow truck 3 hours to get to me, once he hooked my truck onto his I jumped into his truck and we headed to the freight liner. They were closed so I had to wait until the next morning. I was exhausted but still managed to awaken at 07:00am to speak with a representative about how long it would take until my truck would be fully operational.

The representative told me the shop needed to order parts and that it'd take until Monday to be repaired.

Once I updated The weekend DBL about having to wait until Monday, she booked me an Uber and hotel room for the weekend. The area in New Jersey was industrial, nothing but warehouses, so there were no restaurants within walking distance.I had to order from menus that the hotel had laying around. That weekend was terrible, I couldn't wait until Monday came so I could start driving again!

It was my job to contact the shop at freight liner about the update on my truck, so Monday morning I called as soon as they opened at 07:00am. Luckily the representative told me my truck was ready and that I could come pick it up whenever I was ready. I immediately called my DBL to set me up with another Uber to pick up my truck and get back on the road. What a relief it was to jump back in the driver's seat! I was so bored for those three days, stuck inside a hotel room in New Jersey!

What a week I had, this was a perfect example of how one week can turn bad.One thing about it you have to remember is to stay strong and never lose your cool or get frustrated with the universe. Don't expect everyday to be perfect, take the losses, and keep pushing forward everyday!

Chapter 6
The 9th Month

My purpose for driving over the road was to gain some experience, so I could land a local driving job in my hometown. Time was flying and I'd had my class A license for six months.When I was off duty sitting inside the tractors day cab, I constantly checked job boards online for local jobs that would hire me with less than a year of experience driving tractor trailers.

The majority of local jobs in Miami required 1-2 years of experience to even be considered, so I was waiting patiently for the right opportunity to appear. I opted in to receive emails about jobs posted and, luckily, there was an opportunity as a delivery driver that required no experience, just a CDL permit. The perfect opportunity. It was early in the morning so I knew I would be one of the first applicants to send in my application. Now all I had to do was wait for a response.

The next day I received a text message stating that a woman named Alicia from their human resource department wanted to schedule a phone interview with me. I set up a date and time that I would be available to talk with her. For the next couple of days I watched some youtube videos about phone interviews; they were filled with good information about what to do, say, and how to respond to an interviewer's questions. I really wanted this job, so being prepared was all I could focus on!

I set the time for the interview to start at 12pm. I was driving in Illinois that day, so I made sure to take a break in an area where it was safe to park and my phone had good service.

Alicia called, and the interview began. She gave me a description of the job and the salary which was double what I was getting paid driving over the road. I would be home every night (which is what I desired), and would get two days off every week.

She asked basic interview questions - wanted to know about me, my work history, background, and driving experience. I would soon find out talking to her was the first step in the interview process. Everything went well, she liked me enough to follow up and say that the drivers manager, named Elroy, would like to speak with me. I had to set up another date and time to speak with him. I chose an earlier time, before I started my workday, so that I wouldn't have to find a safe place to park. I'd already be parked, settled, and ready for the interview.

The questions he asked were about commercial driving;

- Did I know how to drive 10 speed Manual? My response was no, because while driving over the road I drove an automatic, but that with some training I'd have no problem driving 10 speed.
- When do I perform a pre trip/ post trip?
- How long have I been driving tractor trailer?
- My background; have I ever been arrested?
- Have I been in any accidents?
- What I'd do in different scenarios?
- Do I have experience dealing with customers?
- Can I lift up to 100 pounds?

And the list goes on.

The interview lasted for about an hour. I felt like I did good, and he told me he had more interviews to do but that by the end of next week Alicia would contact me to let me know if I had been selected for the job.

I waited for 3 weeks, just to get an email saying that I wasn't selected for the position. I was heartbroken. I really wanted the position so that I could make good money and be home every night with my family. I continued my search for the next opportunity.

In June I went home for a couple of days. Out of the blue I received a phone call from Elroy, asking if I was still interested in the position. Of course I said yes, with a big smile on my face, he told me Alicia is going to send me a job offer email to sign electronically. Things turned out great for me after 9 months of driving over the road, I just had to have patience. Nowadays I'm home every night and receive a good paycheck every Thursday. I went through 15 days of training, learning how to drive a manual transmission, how to get the job done efficiently, and general driving safety rules.

I'll never forget all the experiences I encountered throughout my time over the road and how it opened my mind to a lot of new things. I saw different states, drove in snow, and became a better driver overall. *I'm glad I made the decision to get my CDL license!*

The CDL CHECKLIST

- If possible Save up some money ($1k-$2k) you're going to need money to eat, pay travel expenses, and pay your bills during the process.
- Study for three written test you have to pass to get your permit; general knowledge, air brakes, and combination. The app (DMV genie) helped me out tremendously, you can also use youtube as a study guide.

- Head over to your local DMV. Take the required three written tests; general knowledge, air brakes, and combination.
- After you've passed all three tests, go get a DOT physical at your local clinic. Make sure your eyes and your health is good, they are testing to make sure you're healthy overall.
- Take the DOT physical card to the DMV to get your permit paper. It will be valid for 90 days. You can renew if needed.
- Find out what CDL school you're going to attend and how much they are charging to enroll. There are plenty of trucking companies that will pay for your tuition, provided that you'll be employed with them for 1 year. The alternate routes are; pay out of your own pocket or finding someone who has a tractor trailer you can rent for a couple of hours to take your state testing (pre trip, backing maneuvers and road test).
- Once enrolled in school, pause all distractions. Stay focused and use youtube as a guide to help with pre trip, coupling/ uncoupling, 10 speed manuels, shifting gears, and all backing maneuvers. Pay attention to the instructors, get plenty of practice during school, good sleep at night will also help..
- The pre trip/in cab air brake test will be the first test you'll take. My opinion is that it's the hardest test, having a good memory is key. Writing out on a white board with erasable markers all the parts and steps helped me.
- Backing maneuvers; Take your time, do not rush while backing, keep both hands on the wheel at all times, and watch out for the cones - you will fail if you run them over.
- Road test; By the time you take the road test you should have had a lot of practice driving the tractor. The most important advice is to look far ahead for hazards, switch gears smoothly, maintaining a good following distance between the cars in front of you, make wide turns, don't

shift or stop on railroad tracks, and constantly watch your mirrors.
- After passing both tests you're going to feel great, it's the biggest self accomplishment. You'll have to wait until the next day to Head over to the DMV with proof you've passed your tests, then just pay the fee to get Class A on your license and the journey will begin.
- Contact the recruiter you dealt with from the company you plan to work for and set up your travels.

Keep a clear mind, good luck. The sky's the limit!

REFERENCES

Here are some Youtube videos I watched during the process of getting my License.

GENERAL KNOWLEDGE, AIR BRAKES, COMBINATION.

Leonard valdez lessons are helpful for all written and endorsement tests.

Leonard Valdez lessons

SHIFTING GEARS/ DOUBLE CLUTCHING

CDL College, LLC breaks down double clutching and exercises you can do at home to help with your rhythm.

CDL College, LLC

PRE TRIP/ IN-CAB INSPECTION/ BRAKE CHECK

An instructor explains a perfect checklist of the entire tractor trailer.

Pretrip checklist

STRAIGHT BACKING/ OFFSET BACKING/ ALLEY DOCK

Straight backing is the foundation for learning the other two maneuvers.

Straight line backing

In this video they do a great job at explaining the offset concept with diagrams.

Offset Backing

This maneuver is tough, here's a straight forward video that will help.

Alley dock